Internet Marketing For Small Businesses: A Step-by-Step Action Guide to Make Internet Marketing Work For Your Small Business

by
Maurice Chavez PHD

Copyright © 2020

All rights reserved. No portion of the book may be reproduced or utilized in any form or by any means, electronic or mechanical, including photocopying, recording, or by any other information storage and retrieval system, without express written permission from author.

Table of Contents

1. Introduction..5
   1.1 What is internet marketing?......................................5
   1.2 How is internet marketing used by small businesses?..........6
   1.3 Tools for internet marketing 8
   1.4 Taking internet marketing to a next level 15
   1.5 Integrated internet marketing....................................18
2. Setting Goals...23
   2.1 Identifying the target audience 23
   2.2 Getting social online 29
   2.3 Internet marketing strategies 2014............................34
   2.4 Product branding..37
3. Search Engine Optimization 40
   3.1 SEO techniques..40
   3.2 Climbing up the ranks..42
   3.3 Different SEO tools 45
   3.4 Conversion optimization..47
4. Internet Marketing Software Programs 50
   4.1 Finding the exact match for the business....................50
   4.2 Easy Emailing..52
   4.3 Avail the power of freebies......................................55
   4.4 Requirements of the business 57
5. Social Media 60
   5.1 Power of Social Media...60
   5.2 Twitter...62
   5.3 Facebook..65
   5.4 LinkedIn..67

5.5 Google + ... 70
6. Customer Service is the Key.. 73
   6.1 Customer First 73
   6.2 Marketing is not advertising 75
   6.3 Building Relations 77
   6.4 The 4'Ps of Marketing 79
7. Conclusion 84
Bonus Section 87

1. Introduction

1.1 What is internet marketing?

Throughout the past few decades, internet marketing has become quite a large source of revenue for online developers. When 'internet marketing' was first developed during the early days of the internet, it was little more than websites and an email/communication network linking companies with their consumers. But as time has worn on, internet marketing has grown into a vastly different beast. With the advent of YouTube and pay-per-click advertising, internet marketing is now a massive, vast industry through which many content creators earn livings and grow their brands. Now of course, this vastness makes it extremely difficult to create an exact definition of just what 'internet marketing' is. The popular definition below, although true, does not completely sum up just what 'internet marketing' is:

"Internet marketing refers to sending emails, creating an online store or a website to make sure that sales are made and products/services are delivered"

1.2 How is internet marketing used by small businesses?

While internet marketing is undeniably important for larger companies, it is absolutely crucial for small businesses, especially those in the startup stage. Internet marketing comes into play for smaller businesses when it comes to raising awareness about the brand and creating messages and content with the intention of it being shared globally.

Internet is especially used for small businesses who cannot afford the more expensive promotional means of television and radio. Many internet marketing tools, which will be outlined further in this guide, are free and easy to use, which make them a fantastic option for small business owners.

In reality, internet marketing alone will not grow your brand into a powerful online presence. Internet marketing must be coupled with high quality content and a marketing plan ranging through various mediums such as radio, television and print media.

Different companies have different approaches towards making online advertising campaigns successful. At the core lies the fact that internet marketing is related to how a product, company or a brand is presented to the buyers and how this image is conveyed across these several mediums. With the evolution of social media and the boost it has seen in the last 5 years, the ways people, think, interact, purchase items and make purchasing decisions have changed a lot and for the same reason, they are also very choosy now as compared to the ones that were present 15 to 20 years before - they have the convenience of being able to surf the internet and purchase products online from the comfort of their home as opposed to travelling to a physical brick-and-mortar store where they are met with time, location and cost constraints. The need in our present time is to make sure that specialized treatment is given to different sectors of the internet marketing process which mainly include web marketing, email marketing and social media marketing. If the best e-commerce strategy is adopted, keeping in mind the customers' then success is at your doorstep.

As a result of advancement in different sectors of the internet, users as well as buyers are not necessarily committed towards a brand the way that they were in decades past. So the strategy in online marketing these days has largely become replicating the commitment to companies consumers felt in decades past and providing the best service to customers in a timely fashion.

Internet marketing is not as easy as it is thought to be; sadly, it's not as simple as creating a few ads and posting a few listings on forums. As a result of this present challenge, care should be practiced to make sure that the brand or company name never comes into bad limelight and regarded as 'spammy' or 'low quality'. It is of immense importance to note that once a brand is degraded online there is no solution to come back to the previous state and the investment is doomed to meet disaster making internet market a nightmare. The internet community is known to be relentlessly rough on companies they deem to be low grade or illegitimate.

Internet marketing is an area in which it would be completely ignorant to deny the importance of social media. Social media marketing and the related tools are intuitive to implement and control as different social media sites such as Facebook and Twitter support business pages by providing embedded tools so that pages execute the business operations easily.

1.3 Tools for internet marketing

Websites like Google have created tools for internet marketing which not only make the life of internet marketers easier but also make sure that the company's functions are executed in a clear, concise and attractive template that appeals to consumers as they browse and shop on the internet. There are numerous tools for internet marketing ranging from small businesses to large corporate organizations.

Here again care should be taken to make sure that right tool is selected for the right purpose and in the long run that tools also fulfill the needs of growing email listing or text message sending. The good news is that almost 75 to 80% tools that are available are offered by large search engines like Google, Bing and Yahoo and they are free to use. This section will deal with the best online or internet marketing tools that are available for the business without any cost:

Google Scholar is one of the best sites for searching ideas and articles for the growing business needs of small businesses. However, and this is extremely unfortunate to note, many small business owners and online content creators are completely unaware that Google Scholar exists. And yet, it is a powerful tool which is of fantastic use to small business owners and online content creators.

One of the greatest, most useful parts of Google Scholar is that it can be integrated with Google Alert. Once this is done, then the articles, news and reviews of that particular topic will be directly sent to the inbox of the user, providing them with a constant stream of content related to their interests which can help them with their business and provide them with a solid amount of research material from which to learn and draw influence from. Small businesses can get a lot of benefits from this search engine as the awesomeness of Google is unquestionable. The research provided here is the latest and it can also help to develop the brand in a way the user wants to see it.

The information provided through Google Scholar is information which can be found incredibly useful to those who require it as well as save a large amount of time during the research process that can be spent doing other things such as creating more quality content, contacting and winning more subscribers and finding ways to connect with a company's existing, real-world fan base.

This is an incredibly important point to note; it doesn't do much good to just have the content arriving in your inbox daily. You must take care to make use of it and find ways to implement it in your company in a way that will be beneficial to both your company's workflow and, most importantly, your end consumers.

Consider using such articles in your workflow by incorporating the knowledge, tips and resources found on those sites into your company's website. Also consider sharing some of this content with your end users through social media. Although it may not be your content, sharing links to other content creators' content through your social media page is an excellent way of communicating with your consumers on a more frequent basis as well as providing them with quality resources, which should really ultimately be your goal.

Sharing third party content also shows your consumers that you really care about their ultimate experience. Consider, for example, that you are a science website. By sharing information from other science websites (and attributing it properly), you provide your readers with quality, third party content which will be of immense value to them and prove that you value more than just selling products, which makes it much easier to get consumers to click on your links when you do choose to do so.

Sharing third party content with your consumers also builds valuable partnerships with content creators on the web which can convert into them sharing your links and content on their website. This type of mutually beneficial partnership is one which many businesses are found engaging in these days because it produces a stream of content and resources that is incredibly beneficial to all those involved, particularly the consumers of both companies which makes it an incredibly effective method of online marketing.

Google Trends

Another masterpiece product from Google that gives instant results regarding the website or the online store you own is Google Trends. Google Trends is an online advertising service which makes it incredibly easy and possible for the users to gain instant access to the keywords that are embedded in the Meta link section of their website. It will show that online content consumer how much traffic is flowing towards the website and provide them with information that can be used to grow and expand this traffic flow. The impact has the potential to be incredibly valuable, as long as you are able to implement the service in a manner that is efficient and makes sense to your consumers.

The most amazing part of all this is that it is also free of cost and comes with the confidence of a global, professional and well-regarded company; Google. If there is a sudden shift in the customer interest then the line graph is also shifted in the exact manner. For all small businesses Google trends is nothing but a boon. Every small business owner with the intention of increasing their online presence and value should make use of Google Trends as a legitimate, valuable option to consider in the area of tracking your growth and development.

What's also great about this service is that it puts small business owners on the same level of large, professional companies who have access to the same type of graphing functional software and equipment. This allows these small business owners to graph their growth and expansion, learning the peak times that internet users are visiting their websites. Through this, website owners are able to know how to tailor their website content and articles based on the highest level of interaction at peak times.

This is an incredibly valuable service, one that is absolutely essential to any good marketing plan and should be used in conjunction with the other information in this eBook.

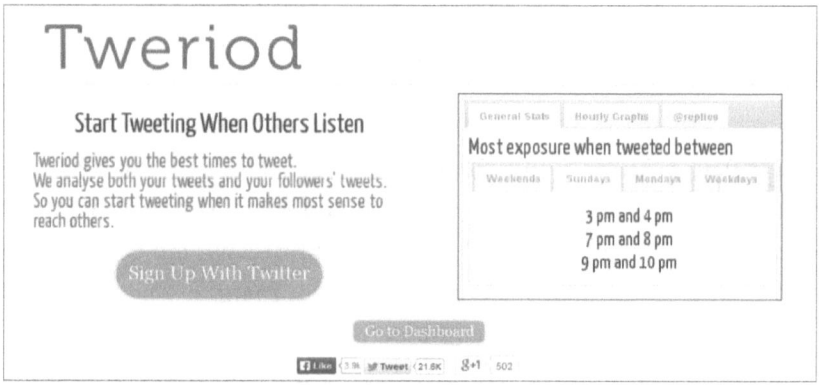

Tweroid

As stated before, social media is an incredibly valuable source of online marketing and should most definitely be used by all brands as they attempt to raise awareness and convert new customers to their fan-base.

On this subject, Tweroid is one of the best tools that shows how authentically an online business or the brand presents itself when it comes to social media in a way that tracking your retweets, likes and reposts simply cannot do.

Tweroid is integrated with your brand's Twitter account and gets the best analysis for your Twitter page's visits, reposts and also generally any sort of interaction that consumers have with your brand's social media page. It also uses the idea of line graphs to show that recent change and shifts.

In addition to all of these things, Tweroid also helps to boost your social media presence to make sure that the best time is guided to the user so that his tweets can get more and more replies. Tweroid comes with the power of Twitter and with 547 M users worldwide it is also a big market for all small businesses.

Back to that second point, about Tweroid providing the content creator with information on the peak times to post and update their social media pages. Far too many content creators and website owners post material at times during which many users are not surfing the web, making that material go to waste. What Tweroid does is provide you with statistics based on when your online consumers are online and interacting most. This makes it incredibly easy for you to tailor your posting times and posting schemes to suit these trends, increasing interaction with your online consumers.

This will grow your business in a way that is extremely big and beneficial for your business. As stated before, social media is absolutely crucial to internet marketing, Twitter, with its millions of users and consumers, is an extremely beneficial place for you to post and share your content.

Wolfram Facebook Report is powered by Facebook and hence it needs little introduction. With 1 billion profiles Facebook is the largest social networking website of the world and hence the largest market for all businesses that have a small budget to spend on marketing.

Facebook provides an extremely valuable way of organizing your brand's content and material - through it's 'Pages' function. By using this 'Pages' function, you give your consumers a neat, organized place to find your content and connect with you in a way that is difficult to do so on any other platform.

Wolfram Facebook Report takes advantage of Facebook's power and viability as a brand launchpad and analyses your Facebook presence through links that are posted, photos, status and videos. The settings can also be modified to make sure that the language preference is set giving the result that how many people are responding from the home country of the company or business.

This is an incredibly important point; the internet levels out the field as far as location of consumers and markets go. Unlike with physical brands and stores, online brands are not limited by geographical barriers.

This is important to note because a service like Wolfram's Facebook Report allows you as a content creator to find out exactly where your consumers are located. This is incredibly valuable because it allows you to tailor your content and branding to suit your various markets as you learn exactly where these markets are based and located.

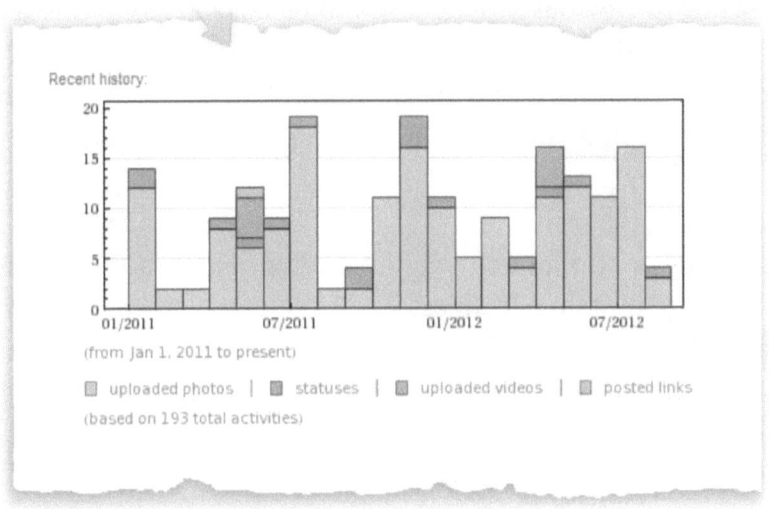

1.4 Taking internet marketing to a next level

Internet marketing can often feel like a bit of a guessing game; unless you're using the services listed above, you likely have very little representation of whether or not your marketing scheme is working effectively. But even after you begin using the above services, you must still make an effort to kick things up a notch and take your internet marketing to the next level.

Taking internet marketing to the next level requires a lot of homework without which it is not possible to execute the strategy or get the desired results and time will be wasted as opposed to being put towards valuable efforts such as truly expanding and growing your business.

However the good part is that any small business has all the tools required to take their internet marketing campaign to the next level. Even with a small budget, businesses can make sure that the internet marketing is a successful venture that yields valuable results for the content creator. So the first step is to spend money and lots of it. Obviously budget has to be considered in this regard and over spending is something that is useless and will create a negative impact. Starting with the website or web store, the image of the content and store should be professional to make sure that the customers are attracted.

Consistency is also an extremely important point in this regard as well. You as an online business owner and content creator want to be sure that your website and internet profiles are similar and consistent in nature. Observe professional brands and notice how they manage to create an experience for their users which is truly unique and memorable across all platforms.

By doing this, you provide your consumers with familiarity and comfort; in recognizing the nature and theme of the forums you choose to place your content on. Consider setting similar profile pictures, header photographs and overall themes in both appearance and content on all of your profiles. This will help grow your business rapidly and will encourage your users to view all of your other profiles and connect with you there.

The second step is to make sure that the brand presence is strengthened. It might take a few months to a year but not beyond that as 365 days are enough to let people on your online profiles know what you are selling and what you are up to. The sequence of online activities should be such that it makes sure that the latest picture of the brand is presented to the customers as it is an advent fact that the brand changes with the passage of time so to keep the customers up to date is the responsibility of the business.

Similar to my previous point, ensure that your online profiles are all updated around the same time. This, again, increases the consistency and provides your viewers with a sense of familiarity and consistency as you develop your brand and attempt to create true fans of your company and your brand.

The third step is really important and it can also be executed in combination with the original business or brand. This third step consists of launching a new product or service to make sure that the original brand is also marketed with the new one. It will not only save cost but it will also make sure that the message is spread over the internet to those customers as well who are in search of the business. The dual effect will be delivering the message in a way that has a broader aspect and the capturing new horizons in form of customers which would definitely help to boost relations.

By launching a new product or service around your online profiles, you also create excitement involving these profiles and make your users feel like they are a part of something as they join and help share your online profiles. This is incredibly valuable for you as a brand owner as you are building new fans and cementing your old consumers.

This is also incredibly important in promoting your brand. As you launch your new product or service through your online profile, you are creating sharable content on your profile which your new and old customers alike will likely share and in turn create more new fantastic consumers and fans of your brand.

The final step is to make sure that all marketing channels are connected to each other strongly. This is an absolutely crucial point to note. By creating profiles that are strongly linked to each other, you are creating profiles through which your existing and new fans alike can locate your other profiles and connect with you in a way that is much deeper than they would if they were just connected on one website.

This means that the information which is delivered on the social media should match the email marketing campaign and the list goes on. In each and every message it is important to ask the customer to visit the website for more details. It will also help to increase the website traffic without any SEO activity.

SEM (Search Engine Marketing) is also a very useful tool in this regard but it is connected to SEO directly which will be discussed later on. This connection will also make sure that the different departments of the business are also working in close relation to each other giving rise to the idea of teamwork as successful internet marketing is never possible without a strong and bonded team of hardworking individuals who understand the need to communicate and cooperate effectively.

Also consider that your online profiles are very specialized and serve specific functions. For example, Instagram is a great site for sharing photos if you have products which can be displayed in that fashion. Twitter does not fulfill that requirement in quite the same manner and as such is not exactly as valuable in this regard. See each platform for what it is and learn the strengths and weaknesses. Make sure that you are taking advantage of each platform and providing a wide variety of content for your online followers to consume.

1.5 Integrated internet marketing

Here's an idea that is even bigger than the internet marketing itself. It is the best strategy that makes it possible for every business regardless of size to get the best results within no time at all. In this part only 3 components of internet marketing will be discussed when it comes to integrating them. These components I'm speaking of are social media, SEO and PPC integration. Whether SEO or social media, voice and tone of writing play an important role in this regard and therefore the consistency I spoke about previously should remain a priority in order to make sure that each message is delivered in same the form with respect to delivery as well as media.

Once the message is delivered, PPC integration will make sure that the analysis is done in a way that makes the scenario of respondents crystal clear.

Social media research and SEO of the website have many things in common. SMO or social media optimization should be backed by the relevant tools that PPC provides to make sure that a business comes to know that what the competitors are up to.

Going back to the first point of the discussion for a minute, it is also important that the video links and their response is added while devising a strategy for SEO of the website as well as the SMO. This will bring much clear picture and at the same time will also increase pay per click management and the ads that are displayed on the website.

Pay per click ads are an extremely effective way of turning your website into valuable 'real estate' through which you can sell 'space' on your site for money from advertisers. Many content creators on sites ranging from YouTube to even self-hosted and owned websites utilize pay per click advertisements.

Essentially, pay per click ads work exactly how you might expect; every time a consumer or site browser clicks on an advertisement, the individual or company who owns that website gets paid a small fee in return for the right to advertise on their site.

What's incredibly important to remember with pay per click ads is that you must ensure that you are posting ads that are not only relevant to your website's niche but also look good. It is incredibly easy to spot websites that look suspicious due to the presence of 'spammy,' irrelevant advertisements that distract the consumer from the original task and have little importance in the grand scheme of sharing your content with the world

Remember, you're trying to serve your customers and provide them with relevant content. Providing relevant, well placed and produced ads on your site using a service like Google's Adsense will help you reach this goal.

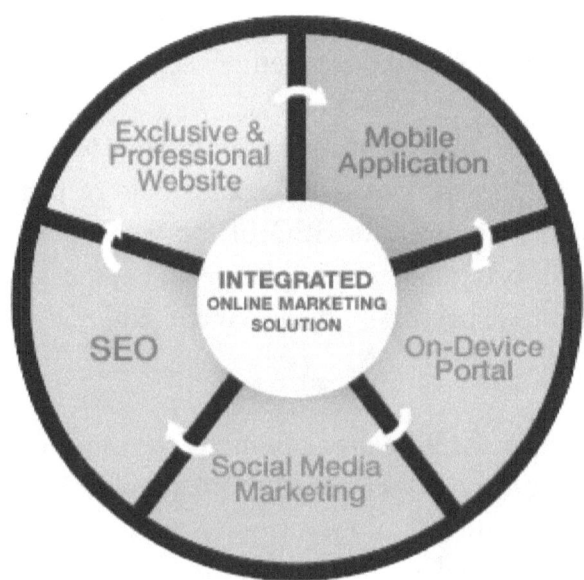

Integrated internet marketing also has a very strong point of paid ads. Social media profiles are the best tool in this regard. These ads just work as PPC and make sure that more customers are directed towards the social media profile of the business as well as the main web store. It also makes sure that ads are displayed to the targeted audience. The best platforms that are to be used in this regard include Facebook, Twitter, LinkedIn and Google+. All these websites are owned by large groups and therefore the users that are present on these sites represent a large population.

What's great about integrated internet marketing is that individuals provide much of the information required to market and brand your products correctly on their own, leaving you to do little more than just research and harvest the information, using it to enhance your small online business. By using popular social media sites like Facebook, Twitter, LinkedIn and Google+, you are increasing your range and reach by an absolutely incredible amount.

For more astounding integration it is also required that your business runs an effective, insightful blog and displays PPC ads there. This is an idea that will definitely bring more customers to the website as well as sales would also increase to a great extent. Apart from covering the PPC portion this blog option will also make sure that the overall SMM and SMO strategies are also devised in a way that is the need of the business.

Creating a blog for your company also provides a more substantial way to connect with your customers than strictly through social media. While social media is an absolutely crucial step to developing a dedicated customer base, social media sites like Twitter and Facebook rely more on 'shorter,' more concise status updates. There isn't much room for substance and longer communication of ideas. This is where your company's blog comes in. Get personal, have several people from your company post daily or weekly blog updates to keep your readers in the loop with new products, services, ideas and give them a peek into the general life of the people who work at your company.

Integrating the internet marketing with different promotions can also bring awesome results. In this regard, the business should run frequent promotions through social media and the campaigns should direct the customers to the website.

For instance, if a question related to the brand is asked then it should also be mentioned that the answer is on the main website. This is a long term process and will prove to be fruitful once a string customer base is established.

Keep in mind that you should have a block of time/resources dedicated to developing social media contests and promotions for your brand. Don't underestimate the importance of such things. One thing that's great is to offer a service/product free to the winner of a particular contest or promotion. Word will spread quickly with the right product and approach to promoting the contest.

So as you can see, integrated internet marketing is not an easy task at all and therefore your business should focus on the goals while devising an idea or plan for this kind of marketing as customers are very sensible nowadays and will likely lose interest if you do not devise your plan carefully and skillfully.

2. Setting Goals

2.1 Identifying the target audience

In online or internet marketing success can only be achieved if the brand as well as the business is directed towards the right direction. By this, I mean target audience; the group of individuals whom your product/service is intended to capture. Your demographic should be chosen based on plenty of research into what various age, gender and race sectors are currently interested in.

This is a task in which almost 40% of the total businesses in the world fail due to the fact that they are not aware of what they are selling and who their clients are. Internet marketing is totally different from the marketing that is done in the real world and for the same reason, the gurus of internet marketing are of the view that spending one year in online business is equal to spending 5 years in a real market.

The integrity as well as the responsibility that is associated with the online business can be judged by this fact. In the online world, a business' audience is not in front of the business or inquiry desk asking for relevant brand or information. Here, the element of trust is something that plays an important role and for the same reason, promises should be kept to make sure that the audience input in the form of cash remains at the highest level.

In Internet marketing the right product for the right person at the right time is all that is needed and hence it is a purpose that should not be overlooked at any cost. Otherwise the business will likely not fare so well.

To target the exact audience is required in internet marketing and even before that it is really important to make sure that these targets are identified clearly and that you stick to the chosen target audience unless the data suggests that you'd be successful if you shifted the target market, which it is very likely that you will have to do if your small business remains successful and stays in business for many years.

Now, if you're wondering why selecting your target market is such a crucial thing, the answer is that clarity in vision is something that is required in any business venture that you wish to be successful.

Targeted audiences are easy to pitch to and get a sale from as it has been observed that in 75% of cases, the target audiences become permanent buyers of the brand, if that brand's products and services do an excellent job of appealing to and satiating a need that the particular demographic has.

Target audiences should therefore be identified in a way that is pointed and makes the picture clear to both parties. Manipulating the facts will not only make the situation worse but will also make sure that audience never come back. This is something you obviously want to avoid, as it has highly detrimental results for your business. Following are some of the points that would help small businesses to make sure that the target audiences are not only identified but also attracted in a highly positive manner:

Know yourself
This is a very important step that also serves as a first stage in this matter. Business should know the answers as well as the pros & cons of the product that it is selling. Your audience will definitely ask questions so it is also advised to learn the necessary responses to face them.

Do not view this knowledge of the cons of your product as a flaw; every good product or service has areas through which it can be improved. In addition, by pretending that your product is perfect, you're creating an atmosphere that is extremely suspicious to consumer who are already being wiser and more aware when something is wrong with the way a company is portraying themselves.

If the business is not well aware of the brand or the product it is selling, then audience will never be attracted. In most of the cases that have been studied, it has also been observed that the audiences taunt the representative if they fail to answer the question related to business. This in turn creates a hostile environment which is generally incredibly not conducive to good business practices and is especially not an environment in which one could hope to ever make a sale. To avoid such a scenario, it is advised to think ahead and plot out the best answer for potential customers and even business partners who may inquire about your company's product or service.

Social monitoring

Social monitoring is kind of like stalking, only in the world of marketing we don't view it as a necessarily illegal activity. In fact, there are millions of people on social networking websites that show themselves openly in the world of cyberspace and hence companies carry out activities of social monitoring activities periodically to make sure that the target audience is captured in the best possible way. Similar to a point made earlier, the real research involves harvesting the data and information, turning it into something that is useful for you as an online content creator.

To do this correctly, it's essential to always be keeping track of how your company's content is doing on your various websites and profiles. Pay attention to whether or not people exposed to your content continue to spread the word through their social media profiles. Do you find that this increases with certain types of posts or content? Try to provide more of that content. Do you find that interaction with your customers increases when you post content at certain times of the day? Try to time your status updates for these times and see if that tendency continues.

Social media monitoring can also be done by going through the profiles of various people you think may be interested in your company's products or services. Look specifically at the activities they like the most, the participation in events and the forms are the most important sources which reveal a lot about the audiences that are available online ready to get a sale to the business.

One crucial point to note as you do this is to ensure that you are exploring the profiles or *relevant* people. It won't do you much good if you explore the profile of someone who has little interest in your company.

Consider utilizing the hashtag (#) feature included on most social media websites as a means of finding out how many people are speaking of your business. Try to create a unique hashtag for your company and encourage your consumers and customers to make use of that hashtag as they speak about your company online. This gives you a means of tracking down the exact number of retweets, favorites and tweets associated with your company's hashtag.

Also note that it is incredibly helpful to make use of existing keywords and hashtags as well. For example, if your company sells shoes, consider making use of popular hashtags likes #Jordans to locate and come into contact with users who may be interested in what your company has to offer.

Grouping Audiences
If the above two steps are followed in a sensible manner, then the output would be a fairly large population of data that needs mentoring. Hence, the next step is to make sure that the people or audiences you've researched and gathered are categorized according to their needs, behaviors and buying trends as well as the responses that the business gets from them in this regard.

Here, the overall targeted audiences will be divided into different groups. At this point, you encounter the time to make sure that each and every audience is divided according to type, based on their needs. This will further simplify the data and the process will also become easier for the audience.

In regards to dividing the audience into groups 'based on needs,' you must keep in mind that this is an incredibly important step and not one that should be taken lightly. Many businesses fail to see the importance of this and as such, their online marketing plans fail to reach the level of success that they potentially could if they only paid more attention to organizing their target market into more concise categories.

Shifting the business trend
This is the final step of this section. After the target audience has been identified, the need of the hour for your business is to make sure that the trend of the functionalities is shifted towards the core audience to make sure that obvious as well as instant results are driven with a combination of efficiency and effectiveness.

Essentially, what I'm getting at here is that once you select your core audience, ensure that your main focus becomes delivering quality products and services to that audience. It's no use trying to cover and attract all your audiences because chances are, there are several smaller sectors which are not worth the time, effort and resources involved in developing products, services and marketing plans to target those specific groups. And so, I reiterate the importance of shifting your focus to one main group that can provide you with a whole host of valuable customers whose loyalty you can count on for years to come.

Implementing this plan correctly have an effect that is unimaginable increasing the sales as well as spreading the world. If target audience or a larger portion of the total is captured then the company would also find a large number of indirect internet marketers as well that will promote the brand free of charge. For some businesses the whole process might call for a process revamp and if it is the case then companies should go for it to make sure that they get benefits in the long run.

2.2 Getting social online

Social media can be regarded as the strongest medium of communicating with customers in a way that is fun and enjoyable for all those involved. As mentioned earlier, for small businesses, social media is a boon.

The best part is that the presence of large quantities of people on all social media platforms makes sure that the businesses flourish in the best possible way. The most renowned social media websites are as follows: Facebook, Twitter, Google+, LinkedIn and YouTube.

These sites have definitely transformed the way people think and respond towards a particular product or service. It is all because of the prevalence of social media in modern society that successful businesses in the world are capturing more and more customers that are not only loyal towards a brand but also make sure that they are getting the best deals as well and spreading the word about a particular company they have discovered and become loyal to. The business pages of such companies are full of videos, promos as well as pictures that deliver messages in an efficient manner; take note of such efforts and ensure that your company is following suit as you attempt to accomplish the very same thing that these larger companies have done; achieving a heightened state of awareness about your company and creating valuable partnerships with plenty of customers and consumers who will be able to take your business to the next level as they engage actively with the various types of content that you produce and share on your social media and self-owned websites. It is also to be noted that social media has been ranked as the best online marketing tool by the most renowned organizations of the world in the area of online brand development and online marketing.

It is therefore an advent fact that social media has transformed the way of doing online businesses - this is a truth that has become so accepted as truth that it's almost laughable that I make a point of mentioning it several times in this book. But that's how crucial it is to success in the online marketing world; I cannot stress the importance of building up profiles on the above networks, starting as soon as you can. Be a dedicated member of each website, dedicate your time and effort to creating content on each of these websites and learning a little bit about the customers you may encounter there and how you may establish contact and turn them into paying, interested individuals.

When it comes to small businesses, the advantages or the benefits are uncountable and for the same reason all small businesses should make a strong business page with a complete profile to make sure that customers get all the answers by reading the page's description. Of course, there will be a few things that aren't quite made as clear. As mentioned previously, you should plan for these situations and rehearse the response that you and your associates will take when the situation arises that a potential customer or business partner asks a question that is not included on your website or in your instructional material.

As mentioned earlier, internet marketing is not necessarily an easy phenomenon at all. Therefore it is also a fact that internet market as a whole with all the important components cannot be carried out by a single person. It should be a team effort where each and every member makes sure that the social media policy that is devised for the business is up to code. This is how it is done at large, professional companies and this is how it should be done at yours. Even if you are not able to hire the specialized staff required for such an effort, consider encouraging your existing employees to research and learn about all the various matters of social media marketing so that they in turn can become a valuable member of your social media team and assist you as you try to bring your brand and company to the next level of success.

There are some points that are very important in this regard and therefore, before starting a social media campaign let's have a look at the different factors that can influence the social media marketing of a business in a highly positive or negative manner depending upon the way of execution:

Taking the first step
It is of utmost importance to make sure that the social media strategy is devised for the business, making sure that the game is played according to the rules and the social media norms are also followed.

Take advantage of the social media norms by keeping your eyes open and paying attention to what's going on where these social media sites are concerned. There are often trends that go 'viral' and by playing by these rules, you demonstrate to those who follow you that you are very much in touch with the norms of the platform and take your venture there seriously. This is absolutely crucial, as your online marketing effort will reek of insincerity if you do not try your best to take the venture seriously and provide a clear, confident image of yourself to your customers and potential customers.

On a similar note, for a small business, the strategy should focus on promoting the brand in a way that is legit. This first step is actually a stepping stone upon which the castle of a great business should be built so it is also very important to erect this stone in a right manner so that the remaining portions are in an orderly fashion.

Creating a brand page
The brand page of the business should be professional and therefore the business page must use the colors that are light in appearance or otherwise reflect the colors of your company. This is a means through which you can achieve that continuity and consistency that I mentioned briefly previously. To reiterate again, this creates an experience for those who come across your site that they will remember as consistent and feel right at home when they enter your profile if they are familiar with your presence on other profiles and websites.

The page title should be the company name and the description should make sure that the company as well as the main brand is defined in a way that answers almost all the questions of the customers. It is also worth considering that the brand page should be made in a way that engages the audience in a way that is required by the business for building new customers and partnerships.

As far as engaging the audience, things like polls and posts which ask the reader to respond directly and leave their thoughts on your page are an extremely valuable source through which to provide engaging content for your social media followers. Things like videos and other sharable content are also extremely valuable.

Hiring a consultant
While this is undeniably a large cost which many small businesses will simply not be able to afford, it is important to hire a specified net head to make sure that all the policies and procedures that are related to the online business are functioning as they should and the company is progressing and growing as it should be. It is really a simple step and the person employed in this regard should have the knowledge related to the norms of social media and this can also be regarded as the core social media knowledge.

When hiring this consultant, also consider that you should hire someone who is very much in tune with what your company is all about and is able to create content that will reflect your company's values and way of conducting business. There is no use hiring someone who will write your status updates and connect with your followers in a way that you as the business owner and company would not; avoid this and try to ensure that your net head is in a position to not only do research on your company before doing any online work but also that they are someone who is able to replicate this tone and attitude towards business.

Learning the rules
This is all related to law of presence on social media and it should make sure that the business never uses the tools of false or fake campaigns to manipulate the customers nor shall it use anything that is not related to the brand pretending that the product has those qualities.

If these rules are not followed then the results could be fatal and the penalties are page and social media presence ban.

What's more than the presence ban is that by creating false advertising and profiles, you're creating an environment through which your customers will judge your ability to conduct business and your business practices in general. If you are willing to lie about the very nature of your products, what's to say that you won't lie about your warranty policy or otherwise defraud your customers and partners? This is a quick way to get your company labelled as a 'scam,' which is a virtually impossible label to get rid of. Do the right thing and be honest in your marketing and social media presence it will help you greatly in the long run.

Here are some interesting facts about social media:

- **The total number of users of Facebook is 1 billion and the growth rate is 8% per annum.**
- **The total users of Twitter are 554M and 77% of the top companies are there on this platform.**
- **The total users of Google+ are 540M with a growth of 17% per annum.**
- **The total length of all the videos that have been seen on YouTube till now is 10000 years.**

It is just a small part so small business can easily imagine what would be taste of the whole cake.

2.3 Internet marketing strategies 2014

This is a phenomenon that is based in certain predictions which are very important as we are almost saying goodbye to 2014. This year saw a boom in the internet marketing industry and all the related strategies that earned considerable revenue for the firms carrying this business. Content marketing is regarded as a part of internet marketing and this field also saw an expansion with a growth rate of 8% in the year 2014.

This is incredible growth in an industry that is already booming. Experts predict that this growth will continue far into the future, creating an environment that is especially conducive to and rewarding of companies that take advantage of the global, cultural and economic phenomenon that is the World Wide Web.

Now, many successful companies are also shifting focus from TV and media towards the inbound selling strategies that have proven to be fruitful. The other side of the picture shows totally opposite results and it is to be noted that the content marketing strategies have not proven to be a savior for the businesses. According to Business Insider only 14% of the total businesses reported that the content marketing strategy has proven to be the best or at least it has worked.

The other factor that will affect the success of internet marketing and the strategies that are related is the lack of education hence forcing the businesses to look for new horizons to make sure that they effectively reach the targets for this year. Companies are also blaming the people they claim they needed to get the job done are not present and it has proven to be a major setback for all the businesses that are relying on internet marketing to promote their messages.

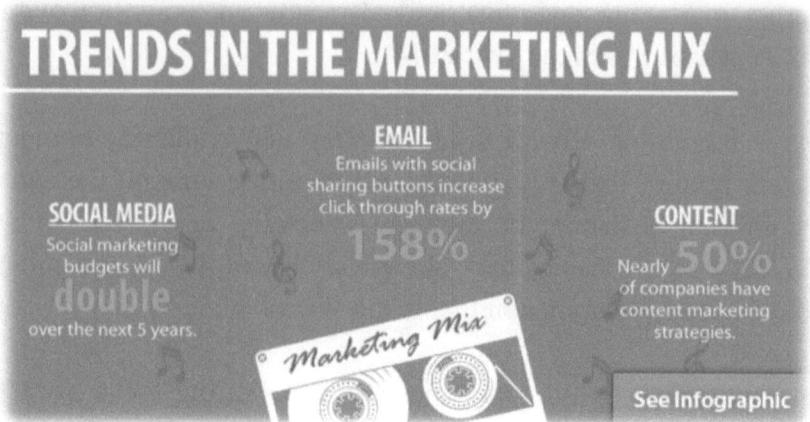

Social media, which has also been mentioned by Forbes in the list of most effective online marketing tools, has been second on the list of internet marketing strategies.

According to the experts of the internet marketing industry, it is really important for businesses to go through their social media policy which will make sure that the overall strategy is revamped if they want to meet the challenges of the year 2015, as well as the many years that are yet to come.

Social media is far beyond the traditional marketing campaigns such as posting videos and photos only. Experts are of the view that the modern consumers of 2015 want to see diversity in the output of companies on social media as well as the related mediums that are provided by the sites to promote businesses.

The next point supports all those who are using image centric content to promote the business. During the current year it has been reported that the use of images has increased up to 70% and marketers have also examined a positive response in this regard. It has another meaning which clearly shows that the image centric social media platforms such as Pintrest and Instagram will rule in the coming days.

Using well designed and placed images in your company's social media profiles as well as blog posts will make sure that the maximum customers are attracted towards the core business brand as well as the way of operations showing a healthy business growth. Overall the strategy in the year 2014 was not in line with the strategy of the previous year at all and same goes for the coming year as well.

What makes pictures such a popular medium with consumers is that they do not take much effort to look at and enjoy. Whereas articles and blog posts must be read to be effective, you as a business owner can take a picture of a product related to your company and have it be spread across the entire world through your social media profiles on sites like Instagram.

2.4 Product branding

It is a fact that in the world of today, internet marketing for small businesses has seen new heights and it is now clear that internet marketing = brand awareness. Most of the B2B marketers who work for small businesses are of the view that the way a brand is presented to the customer is equal to the first meeting with the customer and the fact is that it is really important is to make sure that this first meeting creates a maximum impact on the customer as well as it is also very important in closing a sale.

The old adage still stands; first impressions are crucial. These are the defining moments of your brand and they will stick with your company whether you fail miserably or succeed triumphantly.

For product branding, the most important factor for a small business is to know what the price point to attract customers is, in other words, it is really important to make sure that the product is known by the B2B marketer in full otherwise branding could become a nightmare as well. The factors that are related to product branding as well as the overall impact creation are all such that they require the small business to do some modifications in order to make sure that they get the best results.

The first step that a small business should take in this regard should make sure that the website is revamped or at least modified to make sure that the user view becomes optimistic. It is the most important tool that would lead the business to lead the product towards a successful branding. Content marketing is the other tool that is not only cost effective but also makes sure that quality content reaches the customers within time. It will spread the message and will also make it possible that awareness is created among the general public regarding the brand.

Video marketing is also a tool that is not only made for the small businesses but it also makes sure that message is delivered to the targeted audience as well as the customer promoting the brand in a manner that is the need of the time. The best platforms for video marketing are YouTube, Vimeo and Metacafe. These are some of the sites that make it possible for the small business to get into the limelight and to make sure that the brand is presented to the targeted audience in a positive manner.

Today customers not only want to know about the brands but they are also interested in the company backing them so press release marketing or campaign can also be carried out as a part of content marketing strategy. The press release marketing will bring greater visibility to the brand as well as the business that is operating from behind. If press release it exceptionally written then it might become a part of Google News so it means that additional coverage is get without spending a single penny extra.

3. Search Engine Optimization

3.1 SEO techniques

SEO stands for search engine optimization for small businesses it is just like climbing up the ladder of the Google and the other renowned search engines. To make the phenomenon effective it is advised to all small businesses to follow some basic SEO tips and tricks that have been launched in the year 2014 to make sure that the complexity of the idea does not become a headache for them. It will increase the ranking of the website and will make sure that targeted keywords become the best choice of all times. The SEO of any website is based in the fact that keyword planning is done in such a way that makes it possible for all the small businesses to effectively optimize the Google search engine tools as well. Keyword analysis is therefore the first thing that is required in this regard to make the SEO campaign most efficient and effective. The technique that is the best for small businesses is to sign up for Google Keyword planner which is reliable and provides those features which many paid SEO tools never offer. Beside that it is backed by the power of Google which drives 90% if traffic to all the websites of the world. This planner will make sure that keyword phrases are randomly generated for the business so that the latest additions are made to the META tag of the website.

Unfortunately most of the businesses of the internet world make use of or try to optimize one keyword which is a wrong practice especially for the small businesses as they have put their entire investment at stake and in most of the cases they have nothing to back their operations. So for all these businesses it is required to get a group of keywords that are *less competitive and the search rate is also high* this is the most crucial part of the SEO. The small business in this regard can also choose to or opt for the key phrases to make sure that they get the results that are according to their will.

Both off page and on page SEO makes it possible for the small business to improve the rankings and hence a highly talented SEO analyst is requires in this regard making sure that keyword grouping and analysis is done in the best interest of the business. On page optimization also allows the businesses to get quality content so this part s also relevant to the content marketing techniques that are prevailing in the year 2014.

Off page SEO requires a business to make sure that quality links that are also referred to as back links are built. Large and relevant websites can also be used in this regard to make sure that traffic is driven in a legit way. For all small businesses it is required to create a page on Wikipedia as this website is a blessing for all small businesses and above all it is free of cost. Once a back link has been created then driving traffic towards the website is not a hard job to perform. In a nutshell SEO is a process to make sure that the website gets more and more users and this is done with the help of white hat SEO techniques. Legit ways never include black hat SEO techniques as it can result in penalty as well as a ban till the optimization is not back on track.

The last and the most important point in this regard is to make sure that SEO of the website is audited with the help of any external expert to get an insight of what is happening and if there is something wrong how to get a quick fixture.

3.2 Climbing up the ranks

This process also requires a small business to release full energy as the task is not simple at all. The most important research in this regard has been conducted by Hub Spot and they are of the view that 89% of the users all around the world conduct a thorough search online before making any purchase. It is therefore very important for all the businesses to make sure that they are on the first page of the Google search result, top or bottom doesn't matter at all.

A good strategy for the small business includes the fact that a good inbound marketing team is also available for help so that the leads can be converted to sales. SEO or climbing up the ranks never means that you get the sale easily. It is therefore advised to all the businesses especially the small ones to make sure that the SEO strategy gets the best result with the help of inbound marketing. Climbing up the ranks also make sure that the overall strategies are developed in a way that makes it possible for the smaller business to target or focus on the keywords that are related to their core brand as well as the operations. Generic keywords are never an option so it is advised that instead of looking for SEO concentrate in the keywords like "James SEO services".

Once the keywords are fully chosen then come the step of implementing them to the website so that they get the response accordingly. Following are some tips in this regard:

- **Page title should be less than 70 characters.**

- Meta description in the head tag of the website should be less than 155 characters. The ideal approach in this regard is keeping the length in between 150 to 153.

- Alt text is very important for optimization of the website of the small business. It means that each and every image in the website should have a title.

- All the keywords that are mentioned in the Meta tag are also to be included in the website text in bold format.

These are the simple tips and tricks that small businesses can use to improve the incoming traffic and converting the visitors into customers.

The next step is making a blog so it is all about following the blog strategy that drives traffic towards the website. Blogger is a tool that is provided by Google and it allows all the businesses to make blogs free of charge. This service could be used to maximize the SEO benefits that the website is currently enjoying.

The final and the most important step is to repeat the strategy again. SEO is not a strategy that is deployed and then forgotten. It is a crucial step for all small businesses of the world and therefore it requires the business owners to make sure that they are getting the best deals.

Repeating the SEO strategy means that the business periodically reviews all the tools that it is using to optimize the website ranking and therefore it is very important to review all of these tools so that SEO can be driven in the right direction. Without good SEO metrics and tools it is just like optimizing the website with the blindfold on. It will ever get the business to the desired rank and therefore allow all the free SEO tools to help the business optimizing the website. Nothing is perfect in the world of internet and therefore this phenomenon is also applied to the SEO techniques being used. Small businesses should always remember that moving forward is the best path to opt and therefore these metrics will help to remove the areas of weaknesses.

3.3 Different SEO tools

There are tens of thousands of programs that are related to SEO and make sure that website is getting the presence it requires. Being the largest search engine of the world Google has lot to offer to all the clients worldwide and therefore it is really important to make sure that the tools used by small businesses are the one that are backed by the power and might of Google. Below mentioned are some of the tools that Google has developed over the passage of time. For all small businesses using any one of all of these tools will be the best strategy when it comes to internet and online marketing:

Google webmaster
If a small business with a low budget wants to use only one tool for making SEO campaign a success then Google webmaster is the best and only choice. Running this tool with the SEO optimization of the website will make sure that all the broken links are reported, errors fixed and if there is any penalty it is also reported to the site administrators and owners. This tool peeks into the site from an SEO perspective and therefore it makes sure that the issues are resolved.

Google Analytics
This tool is being developed by the Google with every passing day. It makes sure that the complete analysis of the website including the keyword search as well as the analysis of the aspect that are related to Meta tag is done in a very professional manner. As it is a

Google product so nothing matches it however this tool is now increasing competition from the other tools such as Web Trend and Omniture.

Google Ad words
This tool has also been developed to make sure that the user is getting the information related to the keywords and the ones that are commonly in use. Typical SEO campaigns for a small business might find the keywords or the tool bore as in the initial stages the keywords do not generate much traffic and therefore SEO campaign is thought to have failed but this is not the case. The addition of PPC has brought a lot of confidence to all the users of this tool making sure that they are getting the best out of it in relation to SEO. It is advised by the makers not to rely for the exact keyword count in this regard.

Google Consumer Surveys
It is the best tool to monitor whether the site is up to the satisfaction criteria of the users. Google consumer surveys also make sure that the website is modified according to the needs and demands of the users making it a better online marketing place. Actual surveys if conducted through a third party cost a healthy amount of money and therefore it is never advised to go for them as in most of the cases they are not reliable and when it comes to small businesses they are not ready to afford them due to the budget constraints. This tool is powerful to measure the site alteration and modification. For all small businesses it is also advised to run this tool of the site s newly launched.

Google Keyword Planner
This is the most important tool that makes sure that small businesses get the maximum advantage from their online marketplace. This tool makes sure that the exact traffic that has been generated by the use of different keywords is presented in

form of graph and therefore allows the business to make necessary modification. This tool is also very important to make sure that the history of a keyword along with the related searches that have been conducted is shown. This tool is also a good choice to search the keyword functioning according to the language and country.

3.4 Conversion optimization

In very simple words conversion optimization is to make sure each and every person visiting the site becomes a permanent customer. However it is also to be noted that conversion optimization is something that is related to getting the right person on the site so it is relatively easy to convert him. Basic conversion strategy includes a testing phase before the website is formally launched. If there is a flaw in the testing of the user interest then conversion optimization is carried out to detect the flaw and remove it. However this mechanism is very complex even more than the original SEO strategy. Most of the businesses never know that what the point is through which they should enter the mainstream of the conversion optimization and therefore they are confused and hence the testing phase of the plan also fails.

The other part that is related to the conversion optimization is to make sure that leads that are received are the most relevant ones so another aspect of conversion optimization is to make sure that the overall SEO strategy is devised in such a way that it makes it possible for the small businesses to get the sales in a relatively easy manner. There are certain points that are very much related to the conversion optimization of the site as well as of the customers and without complying with these policies conversion optimization will definitely fail.

First point in this regard is to make sure that the people who are hired for the task are those having plenty of experience as well as insight of the business. If people that are related to the process are not well trained then it is very difficult to get the goal which the business requires. With the right choice of people as well as the experience business will know that what the product is offering without which the visitors cannot live and once it has been done it is relatively easy to optimize the customers and this is only possible if the people backing this strategy are experienced and well versed in this form of marketing. So this point of must having experience is very important which backs all the operations related to the methodology.

The right path to carry out successful conversion optimization is to make sure that all those parts of the website are analyzed that a user visits before conversing with the business and giving a sale. This can also be regarded as a user flow and the process is very vast due to the fact that different users have different preferences before they communicate with the business but this step will make sure that a conversion strategy is developed based in the most common path that user interacts with before coming to the salesperson. This development of the strategy is regarded as conversion funnel and this ensures that each and every effort of the business is in line with the operational techniques that are required to get the sales and the overall effect is same as that of a funnel. This conversion funnel will then identify the pages that are categorized as outstanding and the other group as well that is regarded as poor performing pages. It hence acts as the best starting point for the entire conversion optimization strategy in a way that is regarded as the best.

Analyzing the different parts of the funnel is known as global view and it is something that gives the site owners an opportunity to peek into the operational strength of the website as well. Conversion optimization and the related strategy is very important for all small businesses if they want to get the right kind of people to interact with them and get the ultimate growth and share of the market that is their basic requirement.

4. Internet Marketing Software Programs

4.1 Finding the exact match for the business

All businesses are not the same and this phrase also goes for the marketing techniques as different businesses have different requirements that make up the overall marketing strategy of the business. For all small businesses it is worth mentioning that the overall strategy lies in the fact that the program for which the business spends money is not only cheap but also makes sure that it is cost effective in the long run as well. This has been mentioned several times that small businesses have a shortage of capital and for the same reason they look for the services that are free. Depending upon the structure of the business it is also important to examine that the marketing software chosen fulfils the purpose in a way that is regarded as the best and it satisfies the core business operations in an effective manner. There are certain facts that are related to the right marketing software of the business and these are:

- *To make sure that the business is ready for marketing software*
- *Any software that has been chosen in this regard makes sure that it automates the group of marketing activities thereby saving time and cost.*

For most of the small businesses these questions are never easy to understand and implement as unfortunately they are not aware of

the facts and therefore they end up being doomed. Marketing automation is a phenomenon that makes it possible for the business to interact with the end results which is not possible otherwise due to the fact that the sales processes that are embedded in the channel are usually very lengthy. So automation makes it possible for the business to get an overview of the process in the most efficient and effective way. Almost all the marketing software programs make it possible for the business to get awesome results and hence there are few specific cases in which the company or a small business can get maximum benefit from the right choice which they consider as the best for the business.
These cases are:

- *A very large market for instance software programming.*
- *A long sales funnel.*
- *A website with a lot of relevant information.*
- *Processes that are in place to make it possible for different departments to co-ordinate.*

If a small business gets lot of leads on daily basis then the automation software program will act as conversion optimization software as well. It allows passing those leads first that it thinks as more qualified or easily convertible to customers. On the contrary if the business is that small to get minimum leads then the automation is not necessary or it is not useful as it is developed to be.

Marketing software is the right and considered as an excellent one if the website has some quality content to answer the questions of the customers. There are lots of pre sales questions or queries that customers put in so the automaton process makes it possible that before they interact with a sales rep automated answers are provided to them so that they might be able to find the right answer. This also saves the time as well as the manpower energy from being consumed.

Last but not the least the automation software makes it possible for the processes that are established by the business to co-ordinate with each other. It therefore paves a way of departmental co-ordination as well. For example the co-ordination of CRM and the campaign planning can co-ordinate with the help of the automation that has been set by the automation of the marketing software. In this way the processes become smooth and make it possible for the departments to interlink the activities that they are performing.

4.2 Easy Emailing

Emailing campaigns are very crucial and critical for the business as they help generate sales in a manner in which no other internet marketing medium works. Emailing software programs also make it possible for the small businesses to get a cheap way of delivering the message. According to the research that has been conducted by Forbes almost 45% of the total online purchasers make quick decisions after getting a marketing email from the online stores and businesses.

For small businesses the good news is that almost 77 million businesses from all around the world are registered with different email marketing companies and are getting the benefits of getting the best out of their services at lowest possible cost.
For email marketing there are two options available for the small businesses:

- *To purchase email marketing software that is downloaded and installed at the server*
- *To get a monthly subscription such as constant contact or mail chimp*

There is no one size fit all solution for email marketing and for the same reason it is also to be noted that the overall achievement of the company depends upon the fact that the emailing service or software that has been purchased make sure that the best is provided to the company in terms of online marketing as well as the delivery of the content within time. For small businesses it is however important to make sure that they get a monthly service that would do the trick for them. As the leads are not high in number and the subscriber base is under development so installation or hosting of the software is not necessary. Getting a monthly subscription will save time and cost both as setting up separate stations for the emailing campaign is a long term process which also involves huge costs that are always recurring. Below mentioned are some top email marketing service providers which also make sure that the message is delivered to the targeted audience as it is the business that decides that what the target should be:

Constant contact

It is a service that is highly recommended to all the small business owners as it is very cost effective. There are certain issues which are choice based so they can be ignored. First one is that the service is outlandish and the ways that this service uses belongs to mediocre class. The cost of using this service is $50 for a list of 5000 subscribers and for the same reason it is also a first choice of many small businesses that are operating currently.

Mail chimp

This email marketing service certainly needs no introduction due to the fact that it has the largest subscriber base of all times. For serious email marketing this service was good almost 2 to 3 years back but as their subscriber base grew they introduced new features that are not very praised by the email marketers but with hands on of few hours it is not difficult to get the knowledge of this service. The only drawback is that this site forces the subscribers to double opt in i.e. once through the web form and the second time through the confirmation email. It means that a business will lose those customers who will not confirm the email which is not a healthy growth sign.

4.3 Avail the power of freebies

This idea is also dualistic in nature. It makes it possible for all the businesses to get a strong base of loyal customers within days. It is a two way approach and both are known as "freemium marketing" technique to gain control of the business in terms of customer acquisition. First of all the business has to make sure that free services are provided to the customers as a result of promotion or any offer on the purchase of the product or service. According to the human psychology it is a fact that mind is attracted towards the freebie or the service for which person has to pay nothing. A recent research that has been conducted by Wired Magazine a deep analysis of the fact has shown that $ 0 marketing is the future of all internet businesses. Small businesses can also avail the benefits of the freemium marketing by making sure that each tome a particular item is purchased by a customer a free service is also given. As small businesses cannot afford to offer a free gift to every customer so it is feasible for them to make sure that they offer services instead.

The primary rule in this regard is to make sure that the service being offered by a small business is of a high value if purchased. It will attract the customers automatically who will then remember the first interaction with the business. On the other hand it will also allow the business to market itself free of cost as customer would definitely flaunt the service received which would then attract more consumers. The viral effect can only be created if the customer's level of satisfaction is met in a brilliant way. In the year 2014 the biggest expense for any business is to market itself positively and freemium marketing will ensure that this target is met.

From a business perspective freemium marketing will ensure that the business gets promotion and the effects of the strategy are far reaching to almost every person who is there on the internet searching for a company. Free product or service when used by a business makes sure that the viral effect is created for the business. It can further be explained with the examples of Facebook as well as Twitter. Both are renowned social media websites and offer free accounts to all the visitors and hence they are known all over the world for the socializing people. This is a power that a business can also use although it is related to power of social media but for the sake of argument if we just forget the word social media and just remember the word freebie then the concept would be clean and crystal clear. This power if availed by a small business can have effects that cannot be imagined. The voice will reach to million on a single click, message will be spread faster than any other marketing medium and will create new customers. The cross border relationships will be fostered and the business will explore and even get the new horizons in a very easy and effective manner.

Once the steps of freemium marketing are followed in a successful manner then it is really easy for the businesses to create the effect of self-reinforcement until some stupid or hilarious thing is done to aggravate the customers. A small business can also get the market leadership based in the fact that the internet world of today is a warzone where every company either big or small is fighting to make sure that the customers are captured in a highly positive manner creating an impact that even shakes the foundations of may established businesses.

4.4 Requirements of the business

Marketing requirements vary from business to business and for the same reason it is advised to small businesses to use software programs that are match the needs of the core branding of the company. With little budget to spend it is not about getting the best it is all about spending in a smart manner and the best will come your way automatically. By swift marketing software it is never meant that spam messages are sent to the customers randomly by choosing leads. It means that the marketing software is right if it is integrated with the contact database of the business to give an insight of the different functions that are performed by the business. A software program is good for the business if it effectively works with the contact database to make sure that that all the contacts are sync so that only the built in functions of the program are used and further or second time integration is never required. If the contact lists are manually updated they not only consume time but also take manpower that could be consumed to perform other tasks hence the phenomenon is not very appreciated when it comes to small businesses.

The second and the most important characteristic of the marketing software program is to make sure that it displays the data that is related to marketing campaign running. In this way marketing software should also ensure that the data that is provided to the administrators present the working of any hour of the day that the program has performed and on top of that it should also make sure that the readability is such that even a layman can understand the message that is being delivered. Marketing performance as well as the display of the statistics is a benefit that makes marketing software a must need of the business. Mailing statistics that are displayed in this regard should also make sure that response time, send time, start and end times are displayed in chronicle order that will allow the business to take decisions regarding the marketing strategy which is to be adopted.

Before software is ordered for the marketing it is really important to make sure that the requirements are communicated so that the company making the software exactly knows what to produce. For all small businesses it is advised to get a software program that is pre integrated with the CRM and it will make sure that cost is reduced and the program remains in use for a longer period of time getting the business over the cost that it has spent. Following are some of the options that are to be added and they are highly recommended as well:

- **Click search or tracking options**
- **Formatting options**
- **Scheduling options**
- **Deployment at the server or in the cloud**

These requirements once met the marketing software is then considered according to the operations of the business.

The final step that is needed to get marketing software is to make sure that it also handles the responses that are received by the customers. It should automatically update the CRM with all the responses that are received. In case of small number of responses the update activity can be done manually but where the number of responses is large then it is the effective marketing software that prevents the mailing server from being spammed and auto deleted the emails that are not according to the parameters of the pre-defined rules. In this regard the point to be noted is that the frequency of the responses does not matter. Whether the business is large or small the mail server is designed according to the requirements. Therefore the marketing tool should be efficient enough to make sure that it is never chocked. Smart working with a combination of service delivery should be the requirements before a marketing tool is selected.

5. Social Media

5.1 Power of Social Media

Social media has revolutionized the way people think, walk and even talk. For all small businesses power of social media can do wonders and it is a way to increase the revenue without any hassle or involvement of complex processes. From a business perspective opening an account or creating a business page not only increases the revenue but it also makes it possible for them to collect the data of the customers that are loyal. It is the might of social media that also allows the businesses to get the customers in an informal way as the tone of social media is never formal. Small businesses are tempted to open the account on these websites due to the fact that almost each and every social media website is offering bunch of services to the businesses to increase corporate traffic. The truth of the 21st century is social media as when a consumer looks around the often finds social media as the best match to make sure that the product or service that he is about to purchase matches and fulfills the needs.

The use of social media is to be done strategically to make sure that the power resting with this medium of marketing is fully utilized to change the business dimensions in the best interest of the company. However many businesses are of the view that using social media is just like a magic bean that grows overnight to make sure that they are on the path of success. The reality is much different as social media is a complete science which works over the passage of time and therefore real work is required to make sure that the strategy is a success.

There is no exact definition of social media and it is due to the fact that internet in itself is a platform that allows people to socialize. The definition of social media is therefore redundant. Social media changes the pace, style as well as the cost of communication. The cost effectiveness is also a power that only rests with the social media and therefore it is very important for small businesses as they are always looking for cost effectiveness. History has not seen such a cheap and fast mode of communication with the combination of personalization with the customers. Relationship building as well as the getting the right customers is among the most positive aspects of social media.

If a small business is using the power of social media then it is very important that they get the right strategies as well as the tools that are required to make sure that the brand as well as the product is presented to the customer in an efficient and effective manner.

In the recent times it has been observed that most of the small businesses fail to close successful sales due to the absence of the factor of interest. Social media is a platform that makes it possible for the customers as well as the businesses to build that trust over the period of time.

Blending different forms of marketing with the social media makes sure that that the business gets awesome response and builds a healthy following in a relatively short period of time. The tools that a business can use in this regard are content marketing as well as copywriting. Although the skills that are mentioned require separate expertise still the amalgamation can do wonders obviously if done in a write manner.

Social media is not a one day match as it requires investment not in the form of money but time that is regarded as the biggest asset for a small business. The good thing is that this investment is for one time only and once the business is on the right track with respect to social media platform then time is required only to retain the speed.

5.2 Twitter

Twitter itself needs no introduction as there are tens of thousands of success stories related to small businesses that document the evidence that Twitter is one of the best platforms for small businesses to market themselves in a manner that almost triples its sales within a year. There are hundreds of advantages of using this social media platform to expand the business and to meet potential clients face to face. Twitter is a micro blogging social media platform and it is also the best feature that it has to offer. As each message is restricted to 160 characters so it is possible to remain to the point in a manner that saves time. There are certain advantages that make Twitter the best choice of all times and these are:

Monitoring the customers

Small businesses can monitor the conversation of the customers with the company real time. It helps the management to get an overview that what is the brand lacking and what people really think about the services and the business. The best tool that Twitter offers to the business is Twitter deck that has all the features which a professional business page looks for.

Customer services

It is highly recommended to all the small businesses to follow the pages of large organizations so that they could see how these companies are rendering customer services to the clients. Apart from this practice there are hundreds of well documented processes that are available on the internet to make sure that the people *"who call the company on Twitter get a response well in time."*

Problem resolution

Twitter is the best platform that makes sure that all issues related to brand are picked up earlier and the problems are fixed before they get worse. For a small business it is really important to be responsive and to answer all the queries of the customers well in time. Being responsive is an art and Twitter lets the small businesses to master it in an efficient and effective manner.

Breaking ice

Gone are the times when the businesses used to do cold calling and email sending. Twitter is a platform that allows the businesses to get closer to the customers in a manner that is very well defined. If a small business judges the fact that a potential customer is there on the page then messaging that client directly can do wonders.

New business contacts
Twitter fully supports all the small businesses by providing them with tools that they require to build their brand page. Direct business connections can be found with the help of advance Twitter search and Twellow which are then pitched and resultantly sales are generated.

Offering links and help
The headline of each and every tweet should be URL of the main website. This increases traffic and will also make sure that customers are directed towards the main platform of the business. Social media is a fact but it is the website that allows the businesses to get the sales as all promotional material as well as downloads are available there. Apart from the website the other social media pages can also be introduced to the customers. The best way it to link the Twitter account with Facebook and each and every tweet of the business will also be visible on the business page of Facebook.

Auto SEO the website
It is a fact that Twitter allows the business website to climb the ladder of Google. The most important fact that supports the evidence is that a few years before the search engines use to fetch the information related to website only but now they fetch from Facebook profile to LinkedIn and everything so it automatically increases the Google rankings.

For small businesses Twitter is a place that can do wonders and can generate sales at a pace that is unimaginable. Following the guidelines is the key to success and making sure that business flourishes in a way it is required to be.

5.3 Facebook

1.19 billion...... Yes you heard me right this is the number of profiles currently created on Facebook and it is on rise which means that at least for the next 40 to 50 years there is no chance of any other social media website to overcome the power of Facebook. There are almost 8M registered businesses with Facebook which means that lot of opportunities are waiting for the small organizations to grow and flourish. Almost 2/3 of the total power of the social media lies with Facebook and hence it is very important to grab the opportunity as it will help the business to get to a new market full of potential and revenue. There are number of reasons to create a Facebook page and the most important one is the number of people who visit the website to get the work done and to socialize as well. Facebook offers a wide range of tools to make sure that the small business can effectively make use of them to create a strong base of customers. Following are some of the advantages of using Facebook business page for the customers:

Feedback
Unlike other social media sites, Facebook allows your business to create groups that are related to certain interests of the business. These focus groups make it possible for the small businesses to get

feedback about the brand as well as the services that are related to this business. Focus groups are joined by a majority of customers that are brand loyal and they know what the pros and cons of the product are. This makes it possible for the business to get over the issues in a quick manner leading towards customer centricity as well as customer satisfaction, which will in turn convert more customers over to the brand.

The best tool that Facebook provides in this regard is the *Facebook Insight* tool. This Facebook Insight tool is a very useful phenomenon that makes sure that the trend of the customer base is put in form of the management. As a part of feedback, the management of the business also comes to know exactly what the requirement of the customer is.

Humanization
Facebook is all about talking and genuine communication between the brand and the customers. Facebook therefore provides a great opportunity to all the small businesses to give a brand name and a face to the product that it is representing.

Community Creation
Facebook is a great place to gather all your customers and potential customers to make a community. Your business page can post useful links, videos and options that are related to different issues of the brand or can teach the consumers that how they can use a particular product. If the Facebook business page manages to bring a healthy following or likes then it is very easy to make sure that a loyal community is created that would definitely continue to grow.

Like the competitor's page
Creating a Facebook page is never recommended simply because the business rival is also doing so. But there are two important

factors that are to be followed in this regard. Firstly an absence of Facebook page can cost a lot of opportunities. Secondly if the competitor's page is liked using the personal account then it also gets the business an opportunity to have a look at the way competitors are luring the customers.

Increased customer awareness
Now this point is really important when it comes to small businesses as they are in need of making the customer aware of their brand as well as company. It can easily be done in form of photo sharing, link building that is useful, sharing status updates and notifying the customers once there is any important status update. The Facebook fan page is therefore a powerful tool to expand the horizon and to take the business to new heights. Almost each and every renowned site of the world is offering a connection with the Facebook therefore even sky is not the limit and business can get benefits that are remarkable and incredible.

5.4 LinkedIn

LinkedIn can be regarded as the most professional online social media platform. Most of the small businesses use this platform for the sole purpose of recruiting the best talent. The fact is that this tool can be used to create the best collection of connections that foster business growth. The site has not been developed for the purpose of recruiting, it is a great source of B2B marketing of the business in a manner that attracts customers as well as the organizations in need of the product in an a professional way. The best approach flow is as follows:

Remaining up to date

Consumers as well as the businesses prefer to interact with the companies the profiles of which have been frequently updated. This gives latest and state of the art view to others and therefore it helps them trusting the brand. Small business should showcase the relevant information in the profile which should also include the business achievements that are latest. It will make the connections trust the brand and they will be ready to perform the activities of mutual interest and benefits. As mentioned it is a professional social media platform so it can also be used to make sure that the page created for the company has a logo as well as a page link to the main website. The good news is that LinkedIn has recently announced that they would be rewarding the users who update their profiles regularly.

Managing reputation

In the LinkedIn profile the most recent information related business is communicated to the people and therefore it is really important to know that handling this information in an efficient way is something that is required by the business and it is the most crucial factor of all times. The profile is also captured by the search engines and therefore people outside this community can also contact. It is therefore advent that the information should be managed in such a way that lures the customers in the business.

Feedback

Like any other social media website LinkedIn also has n option of collecting professional feedback and for the same reason it has joined hands with third parties to get a 360° review of the profile based in the feedback of the connections. Another way is to make sure that relevant groups are joined which will also generate feedback based on the public view of the profile as well as the products and services that are offered.

Finding business partners
It is the best social media website when it comes to finding business partners as well as the vendors. The quick search option will bring forth thousands of vendors as well as the companies that the business can take advantage from. The business group that has been created in this regard can do exceptional work as it can be combed to get recommendations. Finding the right partner and vendor within the deadline will save money as well as cost of the business that is always wasted if engaged with disappointing vendor.

Recruitment
As mentioned before LinkedIn is used for recruiting due to the fact that recruitment done through LinkedIn is thought to be very effective and efficient. The platform is flooded with talent and the right way is all a small business needs to make sure that the talent hired is according to the match and fits the job description. It will also save the time of the business which is most important of all.

There are certain mistakes which a small business should avoid to make sure that the best advantages of the platform are enjoyed. First point in this regard is to make sure that picture that has been selected for the profile or the group matches the product. Secondly the status of the business should be there to make sure that people get to know what the business is all about. Social media marketing strategy is a boon for small businesses and therefore it should be used in a manner that lures the customers and not disengages them.

5.5 Google +

With 547M users and the power of Google this platform is a place that small businesses can take maximum advantage from. It is a market that is growing continuously and for the same reason it is also regarded as the second largest social media website of the world. Here a question arises that why Google +. The simplest answer is that it is owned by Google which also holds others renowned platforms like Google search engine, YouTube and Google places for business. All these advantages add a very positive impact on the website ranking of the business. The Google plus account also makes sure that the after the search ids conducted via Google search engine highly targeted visitors get to the Google + page or the website of the business.

Facebook offers likes and Google + offers +1 vote count. The more +1 votes to your profile the better. These votes are also sending signals to Google that what is being posted is read and understood by the clients and they like the content or the product of the small business. It increases the significance of the impact that SEO search rankings of the business increase. With a Google + profile small businesses take command and control of the page as well as experience a boost in the brand establishment.

The profile of the Google + page should be very professional showing the general public that what your company is all about, what are the products and services that are offered and what are the features in a very brief manner. Most of the small businesses are unaware of the fact that the profile description is treated as a Meta description of the page of this social media site. It is also to be noted that the description should also include a link that takes the user to the main website. It is also recommended not to stuff keywords in the description as it will give a negative impact.

Sharing is caring and this is also true when it comes to linking the Google + platform with other social media websites. The point to be noted is that the description of the business page should mention all the links that belong to the brand page on the other social media websites.

The next point is to add people in the circles. It is really important and very simple at the same time. If a business adds people to the circles it starts following their profile. In almost 75% of the cases the business connection will get a back addition which means that person has also started following the business page. It is a great phenomenon to make sure that brand is built over the social media and more sales are generated.

Sharing the quality content and getting +1 is of immense importance. It means that a business is posting relevant information that users or the followers want to read. The main advantage lies in the fact that each and every post that is shared creates a link back to the website and therefore the traffic to the website also increases which is a good sign for a small business. Sharing is the most wanted phenomenon when it comes to the developers of Google + as they aim to socialize the world and provide opportunities to small businesses to avail the power of this platform.

The business secret of this platform lies in the fact that more and more sharing of the content posted by the business is done. A small business can ask all the employees to create a Google+ account and share the posts of the business page as well as add links while sharing these posts. This is the most powerful yet a very simple way to make sure that social media traffic is being directed legitimately towards the website.

Google + is here to stay and increase its influence over the period of time. From a customer rich community to high ranks in SEO Google + is the best ever social media platform to increase traffic of highly targeted users.

6. Customer Service is the Key

6.1 Customer First

It is a very irritating fact that most small businesses never treat the customers as VIP's despite of the fact that it is the customer due to which company is running its business operations and generating huge amounts in the name of revenue.

Without customers, a business simply cannot run. That is a simple and basic fact that you must remember as you embark on your business venture. Respect the customer, value their opinion and satisfaction. You will be successful and create many loyal consumers if you remember this fact and act accordingly.

Beside that when it comes to putting the customers first the most of the companies just talk rather than taking some concrete actions. Below mentioned are some of the points that will make sure that the customer is put first in a way he deserves.

Meeting needs and wants

Meeting the needs of the customers is really important. Most of the small businesses never treat it as a part of their online marketing strategy. Instead of launching new product and services the focus of the company should be to make sure that the advantages current customers enjoy are communicated. It will make the new customers believe that what the product is all about and what are the benefits of using it.

Communicating while listening

It is also an important factor that make the customers confidence that their voice is being heard. And not just being heard it is also being responded. Active listening involves empathy and therefore it should be the key factor while customer is being heard. It is also a great point to collect feedback from the customers and to adjust the business operations according to the majority votes.

Honesty is the best policy
No one likes dishonesty and false promises so it is the duty of the business to make sure that facts are communicated to the customers so that they are well aware of the situations. A business does not control the entire world so there are certain factors that are beyond the reach of the business so if there is such a situation a business should clearly deliver its stance. It is a great strategy that will increase the trust of the customer in the business. Honesty is to be practiced even if there is a fear that business will not end up making huge profit.

Hire the correct match
Putting customer first also includes in making sure that the right and experienced people are selected for the job. Right talent at the right place will make it possible for the customer to get a memorable first time contact with the business. During the interviews it should also be made sure that the person being hired knows the meaning of putting customer first. At front desk office the best and the right match is required to perform the task in a manner that is required by the customer.

Training makes a difference
After hiring the right people it is a duty of every small business to coach and treat them in a way that makes the idea of putting customer first clean and clear. The trainings should not be for one time only as with the growing market ongoing trainings serve the purpose in this regard. Once it has been done then assessment

should be in place to make sure that the employees know what they have been trained for. Proper and in time trainings are the key to success when it comes to world class customer services for small businesses.

It is very important to know that small businesses can only flourish in the world of internet if they put the customers first. All the norms that are mentioned above are those which are practiced by the companies owning brick and mortar stores. The environments of conducting business are different but the norms remain the same and for all the small business who want to make themselves shine it is the most important key to make sure that customer company bond are strengthened. There is nothing to worry about as this approach will end up in doubling the business investment within no time at all.

6.2 Marketing is not advertising

There is a difference between marketing and advertising which a small business should know to make sure that they are on the right track. Formerly these two terms were considered synonymous but with the passage of time and the emergence of different forms of marketing the need of the hour is to make sure that a clear line or boundary is drawn to differentiate the ideas. Although the end result of both terms is the same i.e. getting a sale or a customer but the flow as well as process is quite different from each another and therefore it is very important to make sure that they serve the purpose of the small business in their respective ways. Understanding this difference is of vital importance when it comes to all those businesses which are suffering with budget constraints. The idea is directly related to customer acquisition strategy and therefore should be implemented in the purest form to get the best market. Once the business gets the core knowledge of the difference between marketing and advertising then it is advised to revamp the strategies and to make sure that the track of promoting a product is the right one.

Marketing

It is an idea that is mostly related to internal operations of the business and therefore it is very important to get a grip of the process. Marketing is to know who the potential clients are what the target market is. It is also a deep analysis conducted to make sure that what the customer is expecting from the launch of the product or service and what are the steps that a business would take to make sure that it is up to the expectations of the customers. In simple words it is all about the brand management, the color of the logo as well as the style. In this process business makes sure that all these elements are in line with the product that is being launched so that it captures the market and gets the business what it wants in form of revenue as well as customers. It can also be called as a part where the customer is convinced that the company has the right choice for them.

Advertising

Most of the small businesses consider marketing as that part of the business that is related to introduction of the product or service to the general public which is actually advertising. It is a part in which word is spread by the company about the product or service that is launched. All mediums of communications are used to make sure that advertising is effective. It includes social media, print and electronic media as well as advertising through the deployment of billboards. It is that part of the whole process that ensures that the customers are convinced about the existence of the product.

For marketing in an effective manner it is the need of the hour to make sure that target audience is analyzed as well as convinced after studying them thoroughly. Marketing also includes easy remembering slogan as well as the promotional message that is thought provoking and powerful.

Once the product has developed its image in full then comes the advertising techniques which mean that how a product is presented in front of the clients. As the marketing strategy has identified the potential clients so advertising is relatively easy and provides 100% results if the marketing is carried out in a manner that has made the image of the product crystal clear. All tools that could communicate with the general public are used to make sure that the message of the company reaches to as many customers or people as possible.

The fact of the matter is that though they are interrelated but still different processes are adopted making sure that both advertising as well as the marketing fulfills the goals that the business has set in a manner that increases the revenue.

6.3 Building Relations

It means building positive relations with the customers. As the phenomenon is related to internet marketing therefore trust is the main factor that makes sure that customers located in different geographical areas are attracted. It will make the experience of the both sides profound and more logical. Building a positive relationship with the customers is a sign of good business health which fosters customer centricity as well as raises the satisfaction level. Here are some tips for developing a positive relationship with the customers when it comes to online and internet marketing for small businesses. The theme of the phenomenon is to make sure that all these points are blended to make sure that the marketing that is being done is influenced by each and every factor:

Accept the business differences

It is a duty of the business as well as the customer to understand that all the entities are not the same so they are differences that are to be bridged. Once these gaps are identified it is the business that needs to make sure that they are gaped in a manner that makes it possible for the customer to trust the brand as well as the company. It is the desire of the both sides that makes it possible to ultimately get into good and long term relationship. Most of the small businesses in this regard should make sure that these gaps are looked for when the initial process development is being done.

Give time to the customers
It is the most important of all factors that are related to effective relationship building with the customers. A small business should use each and every medium of communication to make sure that customer gets a response. If one way or medium fails then it must look for the alternatives as this is the only way to make sure that time is given to the customer as per their demand. Relationship will become stronger only if the customers get positive vibes from the brand or the company they are following.

Developing communication
These are the skills that are related to each and every individual. It is advent that every person has different set of skills when it comes to communicating with others therefore it is very important for a small business to know that the marketing or the branding of the product is done by the right person. The tone of the marketing should be such that it gives a sense to all the customers that the company is responsive.

Managing mobile marketing
Apart from online marketing it is also important for the small businesses to know that mobile marketing also emerging as a part of strategies of many organizations. The type of mobile marketing that fits the business is all about making sure that the business

knows its core operations in a successful manner. It is great tool to personalize the customers as it delivers the message to a device that customers keep with them all the times. The success as well as the failure of the company depends upon the fact the how effectively it has captured the mobile marketing phenomenon. Again the point that is to be noted is that messages that are sent in this way should dignify the company and must be in accordance with the norms of online as well as internet marketing. There is a great saying *"People forget what the company did to them, they forget what the brand said but they never forget how they both made them feel."* The voice of marketing should be based on this fact as it is the only way of luring the customers into the business, maximizing profits.

6.4 The 4'Ps of Marketing

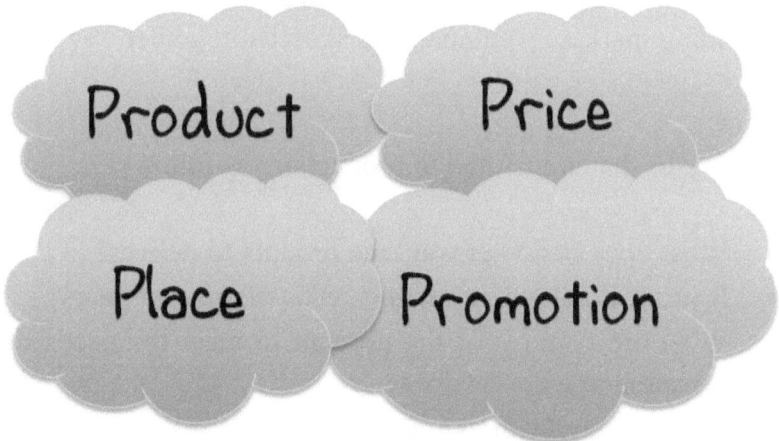

The simplest definition of the marketing is to make sure that right product is presented at the right price to a right customer and at a right time.

4P's of the marketing are all about the definition that has been stated above. Most of the small business that want to excel in the world of interne marketing understanding the 4P's is very important as it is an idea that has been implemented over and over again by many organizations of the world.

The 4P's are as follows:

1. **Product**
2. **Price**
3. **Place and**
4. **Promotion**

There are certain questions that are related to all these factors which a small business should answer to make sure that a commanding marketing campaign is started altogether.

Product
The questions that are related to product are as follows:

- What does customer want the product to deliver?
- Is product able to satisfy the needs of the customers?
- What are features of the product to meet the needs of the consumers?
- Any missing features?
- Any features causing rise in cost and are not being used by the customer?
- How and where will it be used?
- What is the experience of the customer regarding the product?
- How to brand the product?

- What will be the name?
- What are the features which the competitors are not offering?

Price

- What is the price or the value of the product? Is it justified?
- Are there any established points in the area of the internet where it is being launched?
- Is the customer price sensitive?
- Is it possible to decrease the price a bit to make sure that market share gained is huge?
- Is it advisable to increase the price so that the profits margins go up?
- How the company will compare the price when it comes to the competitors?

Place

- Where on the internet will the buyers be looking to avail the product or service?
- If they are visiting online store than of which kind?
- Are the customers interested in online contact?
- Do the customers want to meet the business personally?
- Will they explore any catalogue before coming to the right place?
- Does the business need an online sales force to boost the revenue?
- Is it advised to visit trade fairs for maximum attention?
- What are the competitors doing in this regard and what a business can learn from them?

Promotion

- How, where and when the marketing messages can be forwarded to the potential customers?
- What is the medium beside the internet that would be used to boost sales?
- Is direct email a feasible option in this regard?
- What is the time to promote the product?
- When it comes to the launch of the product is it related to the seasonality of the marketing?
- Are there any environmental issues that make sure that the promotion is to be delayed?
- How the competitors are carrying forward different promotional campaigns and what could be learnt from them?

These are the questions that are related to the launch of the new product in a physical as well as virtual market like that of the internet. A successful business is the one that makes sure that each and every question that has been mentioned above is answered thoroughly to make sure that the marketing campaign becomes multidimensional. It will not only cover the market but will also make sure that proper consideration is given to each and every market segment and the profits are soaring as well.

The 4P's of the marketing segment make sure that the business flourishes, it is therefore strongly advised to all small businesses to opt this model before they start the operations. It is also very useful to make sure that the venture or the amalgamation that is going to take place is in the best interest of the company. To optimize the impact with the target audience this marketing model particularly for the internet marketing can make it possible for the business to start the operation in a highly positive environment with a belief that the profits will be maximized for sure and customers will also response as they will see a company getting the best services and also responding to their queries.

7. Conclusion

Delivering promotional marketing messages to the customer using internet is called internet marketing. It is also known as search engine marketing or SEM. The phenomenon of internet marketing is multi-dimensional as it includes email, mobile advertising, social media and web banner advertising. Large corporations can afford healthy budgets and therefore it is not a problem for them to get state of the art services in relation to internet marketing. However small businesses cannot afford all this and hence they need to seek other resorts to make sure that their online marketing and presence is as effective as that of a multinational. It is also an advent fact that it is all due to the internet marketing strategies of small businesses that the concept is taken to a next level and now large organizations are also deploying same methods to make sure that cost is saved. When we talk about integrated internet marketing then we are actually referring to combination of social media marketing, search engine optimization and PPC efforts to get more customers and to get a voice over the internet in a most effective and efficient way. It can also be regarded as integrating different skills to achieve the results that are simply stunning and therefore making internet marketing campaign a success.

Unfortunately most of the small online businesses don't recognize the power of search engine optimization or SEO and therefore they never hire a professional to perform the work. This not only whacks their online presence but also keeps the website to a lower rank. Online or internet marketing is all about presenting yourself and if the website is located at 4th or 5th page of Google search engine then it is a sure thing that customers will never know what the business is selling or its existence. SEO is therefore of utmost importance in relation to online marketing.

The world of social media has transformed the way customers think and they are now very different from the ones that existed 15 to 20 years back, largely due to the fact that they can now shop with ease and take their time selecting products and services to purchase as opposed to days past, where they had to drive to a brick and mortar store to really connect with a company and build up a relationship with those who work there.

This desire of consumers to connect with brands and brand owners through the highly personal stream of the internet should be seen and used as an extremely valuable opportunity to grow business and provide services and products that people will generally love and share with all those they come into contact with, becoming brand ambassadors for your company.

As opposed to days past, when customers agree to have you post articles, photos and other business related content on their profiles, they are giving you access to their personal lives in a way that simply wasn't possible 20 or even 10 years ago. Treat this privilege with respect and provide content that your consumers will enjoy and find value in; their loyalty and money will follow.

With 1 billion profiles, Facebook is the largest social media website of the world and therefore a boon for those businesses that have a small budget. This is also highlighted by Facebook's provision of powerful tools such as brand pages and full analytical systems which put your small business right on par with big businesses like Apple and Samsung, making the playing field much more level than it was several years ago and allowing you the opportunity to build your brand up in a way that was once reserved for those with millions of dollars to spend on marketing and real-world campaigning.

Availing the power of social media to promote the business is something that works in a fast way and hence it also takes the business to new heights. Relation building and asking old business associates to help is also possible through social media. Getting social requires a business to build a strong brand page on all the social media websites like LinkedIn, Google+ and Twitter.

A small business cannot afford to lose customers so it is really important to get the best customer services team to perform the job done in a right manner. Personalizing the customer priority and putting them first will definitely make it possible for the business to boost sales. Getting promotional strategy, Product, Pricing and Placement strategy in a well-defined direction makes online presence successful that is crucial to business and its goals. Small businesses are not in a position to take risk hence the need of the hour is t gain what they are looking for.

I hope this guide has been tremendously helpful in assisting you and providing you the basics of internet marketing. Take these fundamentals apply them to your small business or brand. You will be satisfied with the rewards.

www.ingramcontent.com/pod-product-compliance
Lightning Source LLC
Chambersburg PA
CBHW031924170526
45157CB00008B/3047